Lenten
Meditations
With

Fulton J. Sheen

GW00499986

Liguori
ONE LIGUORI DRIVE
LIGUORI MO 63057-9999

Imprimi Potest:
Thomas D. Picton, C.Ss.R.
Provincial, Denver Province
The Redemptorists

ISBN 978-0-7648-1684-0
© 2007, Liguori Publications
Printed in the United States of America
07 08 09 10 11   5 4 3 2 1

All rights reserved. No part of this pamphlet may be reproduced, stored in a retrieval system, or transmitted without the written permission of Liguori Publications.

Quotation from the Congregation for Divine Worship and the Discipline of the Sacraments (p. 2) is taken from the *Directory on Popular Piety and the Liturgy Principles and Guidelines,* par. 124, Vatican City, December 2001.

Scripture quotations are from the *New Revised Standard Version of the Bible,* © 1989 by the Division of Christian Education of the National Council of Churches of Christ in the USA. Used with permission. All rights reserved.

Liguori Publications, a nonprofit corporation, is an apostolate of the Redemptorists. To learn more about the Redemptorists, visit Redemptorists.com.

To order, call 800-325-9521
www.liguori.org

Introduction

The word *Lent*, from the Middle English word *lenten*, means "springtime." The Lenten season lasts forty days because Jesus went into the desert for forty days of fasting, meditation and reflection before beginning his ministry.

The Congregation for Divine Worship describes Lent as a time of preparation for Easter. "It is a time to hear the Word of God, to convert, to prepare for and remember Baptism, to be reconciled with God and one's neighbor, and of more frequent recourse to the 'arms of Christian penance': prayer, fasting and good works."

The quotations collected in this booklet from the writings of Bishop Fulton J. Sheen invite us to enter the season of Lent as active participants. With Bishop Sheen as our guide, may we ready our hearts to be "re-created, re-made, and incorporated into the Risen Christ so that we live his life, think his thoughts, and will his love." (From *Simple Truths*)

A complete list of the works quoted in this booklet appears on pages 47 and 48.

Day 1

Invite God In

There is not a single soul at which God has not knocked thousands of times. As the sun is always illuminating, so God is always acting on the soul. Whether we respond or not to God's summoning of our souls, notice that the first impetus always comes from him. He seeks us before we dream of seeking him; he knocks before we invite him in; he loves us before we respond.

LIFT UP YOUR HEART

Listen! I am standing at the door, knocking;
if you hear my voice and open the door,
I will come in to you and eat with you,
and you with me.

REVELATION 3:20

Day 2

Give God Your Heart

God will love you, of course, even though you do not love him, but remember if you give him only half your heart, he can make you only fifty percent happy. You have freedom only to give your heart away. To whom do you give yours? You give it either to the moods of the hour, to your egotism, to creatures, or to God.

SEVEN WORDS OF JESUS AND MARY

*Teach me your way, O Lord, that
I may walk in your truth; give me an
undivided heart to revere your name.*

PSALM 86:11

Day 3

Perfect Trust

In the order of divinity, there is nothing accidental; there is never a collision of blind forces, hurting us, at random. There is, instead, the meeting of a divine will and a human will that has a perfect trust that ultimate good is meant for it, although it may not understand how until eternity. Every human being is, in point of fact, like a baby in the arms of its loving mother, who sometimes administers medicine.

LIFT UP YOUR HEART

We know that all things work together for good for those who love God, who are called according to his purpose.

ROMANS 8:28

Day 4

Purify Your Heart

Prayer opens possibilities. House plants cannot live without water; the flowers will give us their blossoms only if we give them water. Windows will let in light, if we clean them. Our hearts will let in God, if we purify them. Blessings come to those who put themselves in an environment of love.

FROM THE ANGEL'S BLACKBOARD

Draw near to God, and he will draw near to you. Cleanse your hands, you sinners, and purify your hearts, you double-minded.

JAMES 4:8

Day 5

Shine Your Light

Away with mediocrity! Lift up your hearts! The world is looking for light. Will you hide yours under bushels? The earth is looking for savor; will you let the salt lose its savor?

THE CROSS AND THE BEATITUDES

No one after lighting a lamp puts it under the bushel basket, but on the lampstand, and it gives light to all in the house.

MATTHEW 5:15

Day 6

Pray Always

No soul ever fell away from God without giving up prayer. Prayer is that which establishes contact with the divine power and opens the invisible resources of heaven. However dark the way, when we pray, temptation can never master us. The first step downward in the average soul is the giving up of the practice of prayer, the breaking of the circuit with divinity, and the proclamation of one's own self-sufficiency.

CHARACTERS OF THE PASSION

"Stay awake and pray that you may not come into the time of trial; the spirit indeed is willing, but the flesh is weak."

MATTHEW 26:41

Day 7

Cultivate Virtue

True peace has a firm trust in God despite its own past sins; false peace shrinks from the thought of God because it will not put an end to present sins. The only way of keeping evil out is to let God in. Character-building does not consist in the elimination of vice, but in the cultivation of virtue; not in the casting out of sin, but in the deepening of love. The person who wishes to expel evil without praying for the presence of God is doomed to failure. Nothing is secure until he is there and until his love is spread throughout our hearts.

LIFT UP YOUR HEART

Peace I leave with you; my peace I give to you.
I do not give to you as the world gives.
Do not let your hearts be troubled,
and do not let them be afraid.

JOHN 14:27

Day 8

Have Humility

Humility is like underwear: We have to have it, but we should never show it. Pride is what we think ourselves to be; humility is the truth we know about ourselves, not in the eyes of our neighbor, but in the eyes of God.

SIMPLE TRUTHS

When pride comes, then comes disgrace; but wisdom is with the humble.

PROVERBS 11:2

Day 9

Become Fire

The tragedy of this world is not so much the pain in it; the tragedy is that so much of it is wasted. It is only when a log is thrown into the fire that it begins to sing. It is only when the thief was thrown into the fire of a cross that he began to find God. It is only in pain that some begin to discover where love is.

SEVEN WORDS OF JESUS AND MARY

John [said], "I baptize you with water; but one who is more powerful than I is coming; I am not worthy to untie the thong of his sandals. He will baptize you with the Holy Spirit and fire."

LUKE 3:16

Day 10

Uproot Evil

Socrates observed that "people are afraid of letting themselves be cut and cauterized for their healing." In like manner, spiritual goodness can be feared because it will demand a painful uprooting of what is evil. Evil can get so deeply into a person—into the fibers of his muscles, the cells of his blood, the fissures of his brain—that he revolts against the very thought of its removal from him by Perfect Goodness. As some get used to living in dirt, so others get used to sin; and as some dread cleaning their homes, so others dread confession.

LIFT UP YOUR HEART

The next day [John] saw Jesus coming toward him and declared, "Here is the Lamb of God who takes away the sin of the world!"

JOHN 1:29

Day 11

Crucify Pride

Belief in the resurrection of Christ does not start with the fact of the empty tomb, nor only with the fact that dead men rise. It begins with the truth that crucified men rise. In other words, only those who have in some way presided over the crucifixion of their pride and selfishness ever know what it is to rise from the dead. They become "new creatures."

SIMPLE TRUTHS

And those who belong to Christ Jesus have crucified the flesh with its passions and desires.

GALATIANS 5:24

Day 12

God Is on Your Side

God loves you despite your unworthiness. It is his love which will make you better, rather than your betterment which will make him love you. Often during the day say, "God loves me, and he is on my side, by my side."

SIMPLE TRUTHS

But God proves his love for us in that while we still were sinners Christ died for us.

ROMANS 5:8

Day 13

For the Love of God

We would all like to make our own crosses; but since our Lord did not make his own, neither do we make ours. We can take whatever he gives us, and we can make the supernatural best of it. The typist at the desk working on routine letters…the student with his books, the sick in their isolation and pain, the teacher drilling her pupils, the mother dressing the children—every such task, every such duty, can be ennobled and spiritualized if it is done in God's name.

LIFT UP YOUR HEART

And whatever you do, in word or deed, do everything in the name of the Lord Jesus, giving thanks to God the Father through him.

COLOSSIANS 3:17

Day 14

An Acceptable Sacrifice

There is a world of difference between a gift and a sacrifice. A sacrifice is a gift plus the love and personality of the giver. A gift comes out of the pocketbook; a sacrifice out of the heart.

SIMPLE TRUTHS

The sacrifice acceptable to God is a broken spirit; a broken and contrite heart, O God, you will not despise.
PSALM 51:17

Day 15

I Am Poor

So long as there are poor, I am poor;
So long as there are prisons,
    I am a prisoner,
So long as there are sick, I am weak;
So long as there is ignorance,
    I must learn the truth;
So long as there is hate, I must love;
So long as there is hunger, I am famished.

SIMPLE TRUTHS

*"Truly I tell you, just as you did it to
one of the least of these who are
members of my family, you did it to me."*

MATTHEW 25:40

Day 16

Comfort the Sorrowful

Help someone in distress, and you will lighten your own burden. The very joy of alleviating the sorrow of another is the lessening of one's own. If we dig someone else out of a hole, we get out of the hole we are in.

SIMPLE TRUTHS

Therefore encourage one another and build up each other, as indeed you are doing.

1 THESSALONIANS 5:11

Day 17

The Power of Hope

One of the beautiful effects of hope is that it relieves us of the morbid fear of failure….As pride grows less in us, there is an accompanying relief from our old terror of humiliation through failure. Once God and obedience to his will have become our all-encompassing desire, fear of the hostility of others completely evaporates; we are ready to be "fools for Christ."

LIFT UP YOUR HEART

"And now, O Lord, what do I wait for?
My hope is in you."

PSALM 39:7

Day 18

Dying to Self

It is only by dying to our lower self that we live to the higher; it is only by surrendering that we control; it is only by crushing our egotism that we can develop our personality. How does the plant get its power to develop? By being unresponsive and unrelated to others, or by surrendering and adjusting itself to its environment that it may survive?

SEVEN WORDS OF JESUS AND MARY

Then Jesus told his disciples,
"If any want to become my followers,
let them deny themselves and
take up their cross and follow me."

MATTHEW 16:24

Day 19

A Clear Conscience

There is going to be a tremendous transformation of social position at the last day, for God is no respecter of persons. Our social position in the kingdom of God will depend not upon our human popularity or the popularity of propagandists, but only upon those things we carry with us in the shipwreck of the world—a clear conscience and the love of God.

THE CROSS AND THE BEATITUDES

Keep your conscience clear, so that, when you are maligned, those who abuse you for your good conduct in Christ may be put to shame.

1 PETER 3:16

Day 20

The Scars of Christ

What do the scars of Christ teach us? They teach us that life is a struggle: that our condition of a final resurrection is exactly the same as his; that unless there is a cross in our lives, there will never be an empty tomb; that unless there is a Good Friday, there will never be an Easter Sunday; that unless there is a crown of thorns, there will never be the halo of light; and that unless we suffer with him, we shall not rise with him.

CHARACTERS OF THE PASSION

I consider that the sufferings of this present time are not worth comparing with the glory about to be revealed to us.

ROMANS 8:18

Day 21

Become a New Person

You can put off your old nature and put on a new. Since grace is regeneration, it makes little difference what your old nature was. If I throw away an old coat, it makes little difference if I did so because it is torn, or because it is spotted with soup, or because it is moth-eaten, or because it is faded. The only thing that matters is, I throw it away. And when I throw it away, I get a new coat.

SIMPLE TRUTHS

So if anyone is in Christ, there is a new creation: everything old has passed away; see, everything has become new!

2 CORINTHIANS 5:17

Day 22

God's Grace

God's grace is never wanting to those who long to cooperate with it. The will to be wealthy makes people rich; the will to be Christ's makes people Christians.

LIFT UP YOUR HEART

"My grace is sufficient for you, for power is made perfect in weakness."

2 CORINTHIANS 12:9

Day 23

Do Not Give Up

Our occasional failures must not be mistaken for the desertion of God. Two attitudes are possible in sin: We can fall down and get up, or we can fall down and stay there. The fact of having fallen once should not discourage us; because a child falls, it does not give up trying to walk. As sometimes the mother gives the most attention to the child who falls the most, so our failures can be used as a prayer that God be most attentive to us, because of our greater weaknesses.

LIFT UP YOUR HEART

So let us not grow weary in doing what is right, for we will reap at harvest-time, if we do not give up.

GALATIANS 6:9

Day 24

Our Hunger for God

Our hunger for the infinite is never quieted; even those disillusioned by excess of pleasures have always kept in their imagination a hope of somewhere finding a truer source of satisfaction than any they have tried. Our search for the never-ending love is never ended— no one could really love anything unless he thought of it as eternal. Not everyone gives a name to this infinity toward which he tends and for which he yearns, but it is what the rest of us call God.

LIFT UP YOUR HEART

*As a deer longs for flowing streams,
so my soul longs for you, O God.*

PSALM 42:1

Day 25

Love Begets Love

God did not love me because I am lovable. I became lovable because God poured some of his goodness and love into me. I then began to apply this charity to my neighbor. If I do not find him lovable, I have to put love into him as God puts love into me, and thereby I provoke the response of love.

SIMPLE TRUTHS

Beloved, let us love one another, because love is from God; everyone who loves is born of God and knows God.

1 JOHN 4:7

Day 26

A Light in the Darkness

Are you in the valley of despair? Then learn that the Gospel of Christ can be heard as good news even by those whose life has been shattered by bad news, for only those who walk in darkness ever see the stars.

SEVEN WORDS OF JESUS AND MARY

He has rescued us from the power of darkness and transferred us into the kingdom of his beloved Son, in whom we have redemption, the forgiveness of sins.

COLOSSIANS 1:13–14

Day 27

Encourage the Fainthearted

The one who sees the most faults in his neighbor is the one who has never looked inside his own soul....in meditation, by finding ourselves worse than others, we discover that most of our neighbors are better than ourselves.

LIFT UP YOUR HEART

And we urge you, beloved,...encourage the fainthearted, help the weak, be patient with all of them.

1 THESSALONIANS 5:14

Day 28

Surrender to Truth

Abandonment of self to Truth is a prelude to entering into the joy of the Lord. Before a lump of clay can be formed into a shapely piece of pottery, it must first be abandoned to the potter and must lie passive in his hands.

LIFT UP YOUR HEART

Yet, O Lord, you are our Father;
we are the clay, and you are our potter;
we are all the work of your hand.

ISAIAH 64:8

Day 29

Good Thoughts

Evil thoughts are best destroyed by good thoughts that crowd them, evil loves by stronger loves of the good. Evil is not to be fought, head-on, by mere brute willpower; it is better for us to flank it, to drive it from the field by a greater intensity of goodness, a greater love of God. A mind filled with ideas of love and beauty has little room for evil notions.

SIMPLE TRUTHS

Do not be overcome by evil,
but overcome evil with good.

ROMANS 12:21

Day 30

Be Patient With God

Give God a chance. The prolongation of his incarnate life in the Church is an offer, not a demand. It is a gift, not a bargain. You can never deserve it, but you can receive it. God is on the quest of your soul. Whether you will know peace depends on your own will.

SEVEN WORDS OF JESUS AND MARY

For by grace you have been saved through faith, and this is not your own doing; it is the gift of God.

EPHESIANS 2:8

Day 31

The Way to Perfection

God could never let you suffer a pain or a reversal or experience sadness if it could not in some way minister to your perfection. If he did not spare his own Son on the cross for the redemption of the world, then you may be sure that he will sometimes not spare your wants that you might be all you need to be: happy and perfect children of a loving Father.

SIMPLE TRUTHS

*Do not be conformed to this world,
but be transformed by the renewing
of your minds, so that you may discern
what is the will of God—what is
good and acceptable and perfect.*

ROMANS 12:2

Day 32

Sanctify the Moment

Those who sanctify the moment and offer it up in union with God's will never become frustrated—never grumble or complain. They overcome all obstacles by making them occasions of prayer and channels of merit. What were constrictions are thus made opportunities for growth.

LIFT UP YOUR HEART

When reviled, we bless; when persecuted, we endure; when slandered, we speak kindly.

1 CORINTHIANS 4:12–13

Day 33

The Beloved

You will find that, as you pray, the nature of your requests will change. You will ask fewer and fewer things for yourself and more and more for his love. Is it not true in human relationships that the more you love someone, the more you seek to give and the less you desire to receive?

Seven Words of Jesus and Mary

The voice of my beloved!
Look, he comes,
leaping upon the mountains,
bounding over the hills.

Song of Songs 2:8

Day 34

Becoming You

Try meditation for at least fifteen minutes a day, and in the end you will make two great discoveries: what you really are, and what you are on the way to becoming.

SIMPLE TRUTHS

We do not lose heart.
Even though our outer nature
is wasting away, our inner nature
is being renewed day by day.

2 CORINTHIANS 4:16

Day 35

The Prayer of the Saints

The person who thinks only of himself says only prayers of petition; the one who thinks of his neighbor says prayers of intercession; whoever thinks only of loving and serving God, says prayers of abandonment to God's will, and this is the prayer of the saints.

LIFT UP YOUR HEART

Do not love the world or the things
in the world.... [T]he world and its desire
are passing away, but those who
do the will of God live forever.

1 JOHN 2:15, 17

Day 36

Toward Peace

The remaking of the world must always begin with the remaking of one ego. The largest share of the burden of saving the world weighs on those who boast that their bread is the Bread of Life and their wine is the Wine of Christ. The gigantic task must be done in one soul at a time—each single response to grace is a step taken toward peace and joy for all.

LIFT UP YOUR HEART

Depart from evil, and do good;
seek peace, and pursue it.

PSALM 34:14

Day 37

The Mind of Christ

The essence of Christianity consists not in obeying a set of commands, nor in submitting to certain laws, nor in reading Scripture, nor in following the example of Christ. Before all else, it consists in being re-created, re-made, and incorporated into the Risen Christ, so that we live his life, think his thoughts, and will his love.

SIMPLE TRUTHS

*"For who has known the mind
of the Lord so as to instruct him?"
But we have the mind of Christ.*

1 CORINTHIANS 2:16

Day 38

Empty Yourself

Asceticism and mortification are not the ends of a Christian life; they are only the means. The end is charity. Penance merely makes an aperture in ego into which the light of God can pour. As we deflate ourselves, God enters. As we empty ourselves, God fills us. And it is God's arrival that is the important thing.

LIFT UP YOUR HEART

Let the same mind be in you that was in Christ Jesus, who, though he was in the form of God…emptied himself, taking the form of a slave, being born in human likeness.

PHILIPPIANS 2:5–7

Day 39

Gethsemane

No believer ever went into the Gethsemane of bitter grief but that he found his Master had gone a little farther.

SIMPLE TRUTHS

And going a little farther,
[Jesus] threw himself on the ground
and prayed, "My Father, if it is possible,
let this cup pass from me;
yet not what I want but what you want."

MATTHEW 26:39

Day 40

Endure Suffering

Even those who have some degree of sanctity find it hard, sometimes, to remain on the cross until the end; the world is full of half-crucified souls who have come down from the cross at the challenge of the world after an hour, or two hours, or even after two hours and fifty-nine minutes. Few are like the Savior, who will stay until the end that they, like him, might utter the cry of triumph: "It is finished."

LIFT UP YOUR HEART

I have fought the good fight,
I have finished the race,
I have kept the faith.

2 TIMOTHY 4:7

Then Jesus,
crying with a loud voice,
said, "Father, into your hands
I commend my spirit."
Having said this,
he breathed his last.

LUKE 23:46

Also From Fulton J. Sheen

If you enjoyed *Lenten Meditations With Fulton J. Sheen*, please contact us for more information about the six best-selling books quoted in this pamphlet.

Lift Up Your Heart
A Guide to Spiritual Peace
288-page paperback • 800580

Peace of Soul
288-page paperback • 439157

In the Fullness of Time
Christ-Centered Wisdom for the Third Millennium
160-page paperback • 805097

(continued on next page)

(continued from previous page)

From the Angel's Blackboard
The Best of Fulton J. Sheen
256-page paperback • 439256

Simple Truths
Thinking Life Through With Fulton J. Sheen
160-page paperback • 801693

Seven Words of Jesus and Mary
Lessons on Cana and Calvary
96-page paperback • 807084

For prices and ordering information,
please call us call toll free at 800-325-9521,
or visit www.liguori.org.
Please have your credit card handy.